Words to Know

Practice High-Frequency Words

You will need

15 min.

- Word Cards *I, see, a, green*
- Letter Tiles
- crayons
- paper
- pencils

● Use the four Word Cards. Match the letters in each word with Letter Tiles.

▲ Look at the Word Cards. Copy the words on your paper.

■ Copy the Word Card words to make a sentence frame: I see a green _____. Draw a picture of the green thing you see.

D1370864

Words to Know

Practice High-Frequency Words

15 min.

You will need
- Word Cards *goes, kinds, heavy, against, today*
- paper
- pencils

● Read each Word Card. Write the words on your paper. Pick a word to use in a sentence. Say the sentence to your partner.

▲ Read each Word Card. Write the words on your paper. Write a sentence using one or more of the words. Read your sentence to your partner.

■ Read each Word Card. Use the words in sentences. Write sentences using the words. Read your sentences to your partner.

Words to Know

Practice High-Frequency Words

15 min.

You will need

- Word Cards *I, see, a, green*
- pencils
- paper

● Look at the Word Cards for *I, see, a,* and *green.* Copy the words on your paper. Say each word quietly.

▲ Look at the Word Cards for *I, see, a,* and *green.* Copy the words to make a sentence frame: I see a green _____. Draw a picture of the green thing you see. Say the sentence quietly.

■ Look at the Word Cards for *I, see, a,* and *green.* Write two sentences using these words.

Words to Know

Practice High-Frequency Words

15 min.

You will need
- Word Cards *among, instead, another, none*
- Letter Tiles

● Read the Word Cards. Read each word. Then build the words with Letter Tiles. Read the words again.

▲ Read the Word Cards. Build the words with Letter Tiles. Read the words again. Use the words in sentences.

■ Read each Word Card. Build the words with Letter Tiles. Read the words again. Use them in sentences.

Practice High-Frequency Words

15 min.

You will need

- Word Cards *we, like, the, one*
- paper
- pencils
- Letter Tiles

● Look at the Word Cards for *we, like, the, one.* Match Letter Tiles to the letters on the cards. Say each word quietly.

▲ Look at the Word Cards for *we, like, the, one.* Copy the words on your paper. Say each word quietly.

■ Look at the Word Cards *we, like, the, one, I, see, a,* and *green.* Write two sentences using these words.

Words to Know

Practice High-Frequency Words

15 min.

You will need
- Word Cards
- paper
- pencils

● Use the Word Cards. Read the words to a partner. After you read each one, have your partner write it. Now check your partner's work. Are all the words spelled correctly?

▲ Use the Word Cards. Read the words to a partner, using each word in a sentence. After you read each word, have your partner write it. Now check your partner's work. Are all the words spelled correctly?

■ Use the Word Cards. Read the words to a partner, using each word in a sentence. After you read each sentence, have your partner write it. Then have your partner underline the Word to Know. Now check your partner's work. Are all the words spelled correctly?

Words to Know

Practice High-Frequency Words

15 min.

You will need

- Word Cards *look, do, you, was, yellow*
- paper
- pencils
- Letter Tiles

● Look at the Word Cards for *look, do, you, was,* and *yellow.* Match Letter Tiles to the letters on the cards. Say each word quietly.

▲ Look at the Word Cards for *look, do, you, was,* and *yellow.* Copy the words on your paper. Say each word quietly.

■ Look at the Word Cards for *we, the, like, one, look, yellow, do, you,* and *was.* Write two sentences using these words.

Words to Know

Practice High-Frequency Words

15 min.

You will need

- children's dictionaries
- paper
- pencils

- Word Cards *loved, should, door, wood*

● Use the Word Cards. Read the words to a partner. Now find one of the words in a dictionary. Read *only* the definition to your partner. Have your partner figure out which word you described.

▲ Use the Word Cards. Read the words and write them on your paper. Now find one of the words in a dictionary. Read *only* the definition to your partner. Have your partner figure out which word you described.

■ Use the Word Cards. Read the words and write them on your paper. Now find the words in a dictionary. Write *only* the definitions on your paper. Have your partner figure out which definition matches each word.

Words to Know

Practice High-Frequency Words

15 min.

You will need
- Word Cards *they, have, two, that, are*
- pencils
- paper

● Look at the Word Cards for *they, have, two, that,* and *are.* Match the letters in each word with Letter Tiles.

▲ Look at the Word Cards for *they, have, two, that,* and *are.* Copy the words on your paper.

■ Look at the Word Cards for *look, do, you, was, yellow, they, have, two, that,* and *are.* Write sentences using as many of the words as you can.

Practice High-Frequency Words

15 min.

You will need

- Word Cards *along, behind, toward, eyes, never, pulling*
- paper
- pencils
- crayons

● Use the Word Cards. Read each word to a partner. Write one of the words and have your partner read it to you.

▲ Read each Word Card to a partner. Write the words on your paper. Use three of the words in sentences. Read the sentences to your partner.

■ Read each Word Card. Write the words on your paper. Now write sentences using the words. Read your sentences to your partner.

Words to Know

Practice High-Frequency Words

15 min.

You will need

- Word Cards *is, he, three, with, to*
- Letter Tiles
- paper
- pencils

● Look at the Word Cards for *is, he, three, with, to.* Match Letter Tiles to the letters on the cards. Say each word quietly.

▲ Look at the Word Cards for *is, he, three, with, to.* Copy the words on your paper. Say each word quietly.

■ Look at the Word Cards for *look, do, you, was, yellow, is, he, three, with, to.* Write two sentences using as many of these words as you can.

Words to Know

Practice High-Frequency Words

15 min.

You will need
- Word Cards *told, only, across, because, dance, opened, shoes*
- paper
- pencils

● Use the Word Cards. Read each word to a partner. Write one of the words. Have your partner read it to you.

▲ Read each Word Card to a partner. Write the words on your paper. Use two of the words in sentences. Read the sentences to your partner.

■ Use the Word Cards. Write the words on your paper. Now write sentences using the words. Read the sentences to your partner.

Words to Know

Practice High-Frequency Words

15 min.

You will need
- Word Cards *where, here, for, me, go*
- Letter Tiles
- paper
- pencils

● Use the Word Cards. Match the letters in each word with Letter Tiles. Say one of the words in a sentence.

▲ Look at the Word Cards. Write the words on your paper. Write one of the words in a sentence. Read your sentence to your partner.

■ Look at the Word Cards. Write two sentences using as many of the words as you can. Read your sentences to your partner.

Words to Know

Practice High-Frequency Words

15 min.

You will need

- children's dictionaries
- paper
- pencils
- Word Cards *stood, room, thought, picture, remember*

● Use the Word Cards. Read each word. Choose one to find in the dictionary. Read the definition to a partner.

▲ Use the Word Cards. Write the words on your paper. Choose one of the words to find in the dictionary. Write the definition.

■ Use the Word Cards. Write the words on your paper. Choose some of the words to find in the dictionary. Write the definitions of the words you found.

Read Together

Words to Know

Practice High-Frequency Words

15 min.

You will need

- Word Cards *way, my, come, on, in*
- paper
- pencils
- Letter Tiles
- crayons

● **Use the Word Cards. Match the letters in each word with Letter Tiles.**

▲ **Look at the Word Cards. Copy the words on your paper. Pick one of the words and use it in a sentence.**

■ **Write these two sentence frames:**

Come on in, _____!

Complete the sentence by writing your name or another student's name.

That is the way to my _____.

Complete the sentence by writing or drawing a place you like to go.

Words to Know

Practice High-Frequency Words

15 min.

You will need
- Word Cards *eight, moon, above, touch, laugh*
- pencils
- crayons
- paper

● Read aloud the words on the Word Cards. Draw a picture of one of the words. Label the picture.

▲ Write each word from the Word Cards. Draw a picture of one of the words and label it.

■ Write each word from the Word Cards. Draw a picture of one of the words. Write a sentence about the word.

Words to Know

Alphabetize Words

You will need

- Word Cards *take, she, what, up*
- paper
- blank cards
- pencils

15 min.

● Use the Word Cards. Look at the first letter of each word. Place the words in alphabetical order. Circle the first letter of each word.

▲ Use the Word Cards. Place them in alphabetical order. Write the words in a list. Circle the first letter of each word.

■ Use the Word Cards. Place them in alphabetical order. Think of other words you know and write them on blank cards. Arrange them in alphabetical order. Write all the words in a list.

Words to Know

Practice High-Frequency Words

15 min.

You will need
- Word Cards *once, wild, found, took, mouth*
- pencils
- paper

● Use the Word Cards. Read the words. Now write these sentence frames: **I _____ a trip to Washington, D.C. There is a _____ bird in the cherry tree.** Complete the sentence frames by adding the correct word from the Word Cards.

▲ Use the Word Cards. Read the words. Now write a sentence frame, leaving a blank for one of the words from the Word Cards. Have a partner complete the sentence frame by adding the correct word.

■ Use the Word Cards. Read the words. Now write sentence frames, leaving blanks for the words from the Word Cards. Have a partner complete the sentence frames by adding the correct words.

Words to Know

Identify High-Frequency Words

15 min.

You will need

- Word Cards *help, use, from, little, blue, get*
- paper
- pencils
- crayons

● Use the Word Cards. Write the words on your paper. Draw pictures for some of the words.

▲ Use the Word Cards. Write the words on your paper. Use two of the words in a sentence. Draw pictures for some of the words.

■ Use the Word Cards. Write sentences using the words. Then draw pictures that describe the sentences.

Words to Know

Practice High-Frequency Words

15 min.

You will need

- Word Cards *draw, colors, over, drew, great, sign, show*
- pencils
- crayons
- paper

● Use the Word Cards. Read the words. Now write a sentence using one of the words. Underline the word. Draw a picture to match your sentence.

▲ Use the Word Cards. Read the words and write them on your paper. Now write a sentence using one of the words. Draw a picture to match your sentence.

■ Use the Word Cards. Read the words and write them on your paper. Now write sentences using some of the words. Draw pictures to match your sentences.

Words to Know

Alphabetize Words

15 min.

You will need

- Word Cards *eat, her, this, too, four, five*
- paper
- blank cards
- pencils

● Use the Word Cards. Look at the first or second letter of each word. Place the words in alphabetical order.

▲ Use the Word Cards. Place them in alphabetical order. Write the words in a list. Circle the first letter of each word.

■ Use the Word Cards. Place them in alphabetical order. Think of other words you know and write them on blank cards. Arrange them in alphabetical order, along with the Word Card words. Write all the words in a list.

Read Together

Words to Know

Practice High-Frequency Words

15 min.

You will need
- Word Cards *give, surprise, would, enjoy, worry, about*
- paper
- pencils
- crayons

● Use the Word Cards. Read the words. Now write a sentence using one of the words. Underline the word. Draw a picture to match your sentence.

▲ Use the Word Cards. Read the words and write them on your paper. Now write a sentence using one of the words. Draw a picture to match your sentence.

■ Use the Word Cards. Read the words and write them on your paper. Now write sentences using some of the words. Draw pictures to match your sentences.

Sort Words

You will need

- Word Cards *small, tree, your, saw*
- pencils
- paper

● Use the Word Cards. Read the words. Sort them into two piles: words with initial consonant blends and words without initial consonant blends. Write the words and underline the initial consonant blends.

▲ Read the words on the Word Cards. Sort the Word Cards into two piles: words with initial consonant blends and words without initial consonant blends. Write the words and underline the initial consonant blends.

■ Use the Word Cards. Read the words. Write the words with initial consonant blends in one column. Write the words without initial consonant blends in another column. Underline the initial consonant blends. Write sentences using the words.

Words to Know

Practice High-Frequency Words

15 min.

You will need
- Word Cards *does,
good-bye, before,
won't, oh, right*
- Letter Tiles

● Using the Word Cards, build each word using Letter Tiles. Read the words aloud. Use two of the words in sentences.

▲ Using the Word Cards, build each word using Letter Tiles. Work with a partner and say each word in a sentence.

■ Using the Word Cards, build each word using Letter Tiles. Work with a partner and use the words to talk about animals in winter.

 Grade 1, Unit 4, Week 1

25

Words to Know

Practice High-Frequency Words

15 min.

You will need
- Word Cards *home, into, many, them*
- Letter Tiles
- paper
- pencils

● **Look at the Word Cards. Match the letters in each word with Letter Tiles.**

▲ **Look at the Word Cards. Write the words on your paper. Use one of the words in a sentence.**

■ **Look at the Word Cards. Write two sentences using the words. Underline the Words to Know.**

Words to Know

Practice High-Frequency Words

15 min.

You will need

- Word Cards *know, done, push, wait, visit*
- pencils
- paper

● Use the Word Cards. Put them in alphabetical order. Then write them in alphabetical order on your paper.

▲ Use the Word Cards. Put them in alphabetical order. Then write them in alphabetical order on your paper. Write a sentence using one or more of the words.

■ Use the Word Cards. Put them in alphabetical order. Then write them in alphabetical order on your paper. Write sentences using the words. Underline the Words to Know.

Words to Know

Practice High-Frequency Words

15 min.

You will need

- Word Cards *want, no, good, put, catch, said*
- pencils
- crayons
- paper

● Use the Word Cards. Read each word. Put the verbs in one pile and the words that are not verbs in another pile. Draw a picture of one of the verbs and label it.

▲ Use the Word Cards. Read each word. Put the verbs in one pile and the words that are not verbs in another pile. Draw pictures of some of the verbs and label them.

■ Use the Word Cards. Read each word. Put the verbs in one pile and the words that are not verbs in another pile. Write sentences using the words and underline the verbs. Draw pictures to go with your sentences.

Words to Know

Practice High-Frequency Words

15 min.

You will need
- children's dictionary
- paper
- pencils

- Word Cards *few, afraid, read, soon, how, again*

● Use the Word Cards. Write the Words to Know on your paper. Choose one of the words and find it in the dictionary. Write the definition next to it.

▲ Use the Word Cards. Write the Words to Know on your paper. Choose some of the words and find them in the dictionary. Write the definitions next to the words.

■ Use the Word Cards. Write the Words to Know on your paper. Find the words in the dictionary. Write the definitions next to the words.

Practice High-Frequency Words

15 min.

You will need

- Word Cards *could, be, old, paper, of, horse*
- pencils

- paper

● Use the Word Cards. Write them on your paper. Now write a sentence using one of the words.

▲ Use the Word Cards. Write them on your paper. Now write sentences using some of the words.

■ Use the Word Cards. Write them on your paper. Now write sentences using some of the words.

Practice High-Frequency Words

15 min.

You will need

- Letter Tiles
- paper
- pencils

- Word Cards
  sure, were, enough, every, any, own

● Use the Word Cards. Match the letters in each word with Letter Tiles. Then think of a sentence using one of the words. Say the sentence to your partner.

▲ Look at the Word Cards. Write the words on your paper. Then write sentences using two of the words.

■ Look at the Word Cards. Write the words on your paper. Then write sentences using the words.

Practice High-Frequency Words

15 min.

You will need

- Word Cards *down, there, inside, together, now*
- paper
- pencils
- Letter Tiles

● Use the Word Cards. Match the letters in each word with Letter Tiles. Write the words on your paper.

▲ Look at the Word Cards. Write the words on your paper. Use some of the words in sentences. Underline the Words to Know in your sentences.

■ Look at the Word Cards. Write sentences using the words. Underline the Words to Know in your sentences.

Words to Know

Practice High-Frequency Words

You will need

15 min.

- Word Cards *things, always, day, become, nothing, stays, everything*

- Unit 3 Student Book

- pencils

● Use the Word Cards. Read the words to a partner. Have your partner think of antonyms for the words *always, day, nothing,* and *stays.*

▲ On a T-chart, label the left column *Words to Know.* Label the right column *Antonyms.* Write the Words to Know in the left column, and then write antonyms for the words in the right column. Some of the words may not have antonyms.

■ On a T-chart, label the left column *Words to Know.* Label the right column *Antonyms.* Write the Words to Know in the left column, and then write antonyms for the words in the right column. Some of the words may not have antonyms. Add more words from *A Place to Play* to your chart, along with antonyms.

Words to Know

Practice High-Frequency Words

15 min.

You will need

- Word Cards *grow, food, around, find, water, under*
- Letter Tiles
- paper
- pencils
- crayons

● Use the Word Cards. Match the letters in each word with Letter Tiles. Write the words on your paper. Draw a picture to illustrate one of the words. Label your picture.

▲ Look at the Word Cards. Write the words on your paper. Use some of the words in sentences. Underline the Words to Know in your sentences. Draw a picture to illustrate one of your sentences.

■ Look at the Word Cards. Write sentences using the words. Underline the Words to Know in your sentences. Draw a picture to illustrate one of your sentences.

Read Together

Words to Know

Practice High-Frequency Words

15 min.

You will need
- Word Cards *also, family, new, other, some, their*
- paper
- pencils

● Using one of the Word Cards, say a sentence using that word. Have your partner point to the correct Word Card. Write each word you use on your paper.

▲ Using one of the Word Cards, say a sentence using that word. Have your partner point to the correct Word Card. Write each word you use on your paper.

■ Using one of the Word Cards, say a sentence using that word. Have your partner point to the correct Word Card. Write each word you use on your paper. Write sentences using the words as you figure them out.

Read Together